CONTENTS

Title Page

Copyright

Chapter Guide

Introduction

Chapter 1

Chapter 2

Chapter 3   1

Chapter 4   16

Chapter 5   23

Chapter 6   34

Chapter 7   37

Chapter 8   40

Chapter 9   45

Chapter 10   53

Chapter 11   55

Chapter 12   58

Discussion Questions For You And Your Tween or Teen   61

Conclusion   75

Resources To Protect Your Kids   76

Programs To Set Limits, Manage and Protect Your Kids   77

Family Cell Phone Contract   85

Apps of Concern   88

Other Resources   91

SOS! THE TECHNOLOGY GUIDEBOOK FOR PARENTS OF TWEENS AND TEENS

Get The Answers You Need, Keep Them Safe and Enjoy Your Kids Again

Sheryl Gould

with Jennifer Kehl

CHAPTER GUIDE

Chapter One: The 5 Most Common Mistakes We Make

Chapter Two: What We Need to Understand First

Chapter Three: How to Minimize the Challenges (and Arguments): Setting Limits

Chapter Four: Communication Is Key

Chapter Five: Deciding on Ground Rules

Chapter Six: Encourage Positive Online Behavior

Chapter Seven: Keeping Them Safe

Chapter Eight: The Negative Impacts of Social Media

Chapter Nine: The Risks- **Cyberbullying, Sexting and Pornography**

Chapter Ten: How Do You Know if You Should be Concerned?

Chapter Eleven: Gaming
Chapter Twelve: Be Intentional - FaceTime versus ScreenTime

Discussion Questions for You and Your Tween or Teen Including a

Sheryl Gould

Special Article From Our Moms of Tweens and Teens Blog
"Should I Read My Teen's Text Messages?"

INTRODUCTION

Weee have so many questions when it comes to technology and our kids.

At what age should I allow my kids to get a smartphone?

How much screen time is OK for my kid(s)?

How do I manage their usage?

What should my tech rules and limits be?

How can I keep them safe from inappropriate content and dangerous apps?

What do I do if I find out my kid was looking at pornography?

How do I talk to them so they won't constantly argue and will cooperate with my rules?

The list goes on!

Sheryl Gould

If you're reading this you know full well - the struggle is real!

We are the first generation to navigate all of this technology with our kids. We have our feet in both worlds: we remember a life without technology and now we live in the digital world. No wonder we feel overwhelmed!

Whether it's smartphones, social media, the Internet, or video-games, media and tech have become a huge part of our families' lives. All of the technology our kids are bombarded with can affect schoolwork, relationships, emotional and physical health, and concentration - just to name a few.

And if this isn't enough, here are a few statistics that confirm our fears:

Since 2013, rates of teenage depression and suicide have sky-rocketed. It is no coincidence that this is the same year the proportion of Americans owning a cellphone surpassed 50 percent – and the generation now known as the iGen was born.

Up to 40% of children have been involved in a cyberbullying incident[1].

48% of teens who spend more than five hours a day on electronic devices report at least one suicide-related outcome (felt very lonely and considered, planned, or attempted suicide)[2].

50% of teens report feeling addicted to their mobile devices; 78% check their devices at least hourly.

Today's kids are literally surrounded by technology everywhere they go. Smartphones, high speed internet, laptops, video game consoles, tablets and the list is growing every year (some restaurants even have tablets with games on the table!). Even schoolwork is done on their devices which can make managing it all the more difficult and frustrating.

So what do we do?!

Here's the truth:

Technology is here to stay whether we like it or not. We can feel angry and complain about all of the risks, dangers, and challenges of navigating our kids' technology, or we can be proactive. Rather than viewing technology as "the problem," we need to decide how we will respond and what we will do to live in harmony with technology.

In the midst of our fears and frustration about technology, remember this - when all is said and done, it is your kid's well-being, character, and the strong relationship that you build with them that will matter the most.

In this book, I will answer the most common questions and concerns parents have and offer practical tips and strategies you can use, as well as valuable resources to help.

I will share how to talk to your kids about their technology and what you need to know to build a stronger relationship with your kids. You will be guided through setting limits that work, how to keep them safe, and how to get your kids on board. Most importantly, you will learn how to have the difficult conversations and cultivate a relationship where they will come to you when something is wrong or they have made a poor decision.

CHAPTER 1

The 5 Most Common
Mistakes We Make

I fwe can take a step back and all agree that technology is here to stay whether we like it or not, the question becomes, what can we do about it?

I want to share with you the five most common mistakes I see parents make when it comes to navigating their kids' technology. Once we get these out of the way, we will jump in and discuss what you can do to be proactive.

◆ ◆ ◆

#1 We Make Technology The Enemy

"Kids today are growing up with technology, not growing into it like previous generations. This means that much of their learning,

friendships and fun happens online." - Google/wellbeing.google

One of the most common concerns I hear from mothers of tweens and teens is the fear and frustration regarding the negative impact social media is having on their kids and their relationships with them.

At times we've all found ourselves wanting to throw our hands up in surrender. Other times we've wanted to throw the phone or tablet out the window. Or we are ashamed to admit we've wrestled our kids to the ground trying to grab the controller or their phone in a moment of utter desperation (mom with hand raised emoji)!

We are on the battlefield fighting against what feels like the enemy.

It doesn't have to be this way.

Our kids' technology doesn't need to be our foe. When media is used meaningfully and responsibly, it can enhance daily life and our relationships with our kids (yes, it can!).

#2 We Overreact Out of Fear

When fear is in the driver's seat, ultimately it's not going to steer you in the right direction.

We hear all the stories: the girl in the chatroom talking to a man pretending to be a teenager, the kid who was being cyberbullied leading to horrific consequences, a teen addicted to pornography, a girl who was caught sexting. Not to mention, we are bombarded by the latest studies on how technology is ruining our kids and affecting their brains.

Makes total sense we'd be fearful! However, fear fuels anxiety, and anxiety can cause us to overreact in the moment.

In my experience of working with parents - and as a parent myself - I have found that when we feel scared, powerless, or our kids aren't communicating with us, the first thing we want to do is to grab their phone, read their texts, or get overly involved in their business. We try to reassert control.

And what parent hasn't overreacted in the heat of the moment?

However, this approach doesn't work, nor does it help us to be a person whom our kids want to talk to when they have a problem or are dealing with something they need help with.

I implore you, do not default to grabbing your kid's phone, reading their texts, or getting overly involved in their business because you're scared or feeling a sense of powerlessness.

Don't bypass having the sometimes difficult but important conversations to help your kids make good decisions, self-regulate, and stay safe in our digital world.

It's really important that we know the difference between parenting by fear and taking the necessary steps to be responsible parents and support our kids well-being.

#3 We Don't Set Limits/Boundaries

"Boundaries are like an anchor in a storm. We can ride the waves with greater peace and ease rather than being tossed by fear with every wave that comes along. We can stand firm and relax a little. If they happen to step over the line, the consequences can speak for themselves."

When we lack boundaries, kids don't know who's in charge.

I hear from moms who are walking on eggshells because their kid is ruling the family and they don't know what to do.

Although kids give off the impression they'd like to be in charge, deep down they know they need help making good decisions.

Even when kids argue and make it difficult - they want their parents to lead. When kids are left in charge and there's nothing to push up against, their anxiety skyrockets.

They won't always understand why they need limits/boundaries or like them for that matter. And while we might feel like mean moms when enforcing them, our kids desperately need them.

In fact, healthy boundaries create clarity and peace in the home—keeping them safe and us sane.

Where there are no boundaries, there is confusion and chaos. When we are constantly changing our no to yes and yes to no, it's confusing for everybody.

When we are clear about our expectations and the rules in our home, we don't need to hover, be so strict, or resort to controlling behavior.

#4 We Get Hooked in Power Struggles

"Power struggles lead me to entertain the notion that I'd be better off spending a weekend at the dentist than staying home arguing with my teenager."

Even though we hate when our teenagers become grizzly bears and life feels like an emotional roller coaster ride - arguing and pushing the boundaries is a necessary developmental process they must go through as they inch toward adulthood. Understanding this fact can keep you from getting hooked.

A few pointers to avoid getting hooked in a power struggle:

Don't engage in who's right or wrong. A teenager will rarely say, "You know what Mom, you're right."

If they're angry, it's okay. You don't need to defend, argue or convince them that your decision is the right one.

Don't take the bait. It's easy to recognize when we take the bait because we get a little nutty. We feel out of control and, in a panic, grasp to control anything.

I know it's hard to resist the juicy bait they throw out. After all, they're so good at it! I think this is one of the hardest things to avoid doing as a parent.

The next time your adolescent tries to hook you into a power struggle, allow them to express that they're upset, take a deep breath and resist getting into the ring with them (you're going to find it helpful when we discuss *How To Minimize The Challenges (and Arguments): Setting Limits* in Chapter 3).

#5 We Avoid Upsetting Our Kids

"If we're dependent on our teenager liking us, we will feel like a victim most of the time."

Sometimes, your tween or teen is going to have negative feelings towards you, and most of the time, they're not going to like the word "no." Buckle up and get comfortable with it.

One of the common pitfalls I find parents fall into is the failure to set limits because they don't want to upset their kids and they're anticipating a battle.

Here's the truth: 9 times out of 10 when you set a limit with your kids or tell them no, they're not going to like it. Give them the space to be upset. You don't need to over explain or try to convince them to feel differently. We have to be okay with them being upset and give them the limits they desperately need.

Remember that adolescence is a time when they are fighting for independence and going through many changes. Expecting them to be calm and agreeable during such a time of transition is un-realistic.

I know it can be difficult to listen to our kids when they're whining and angry. However, as annoying as it is, it's normal and healthy for your tween or teen to express when they're angry, worried, sad, or disappointed.

You don't need to fix it or change how they're feeling. What they need is for you to be able to handle whatever they're feeling and hold the boundary lines for them.

CHAPTER 2

What We Need To Understand First

This Is Their World

They've got smartphones, Instagram, SnapChat, YouTube, gaming, texting, social media, apps and more. Technology is a huge part of the world our kids live in.

We have to acknowledge this fact and with that will come a greater understanding as to why our kids would like to be (if we let them) on technology 24/7.

Right at their fingertips, tweens and teens use technology to connect with friends, like, comment and discuss things with others and find humor. It's how they learn, have fun, innovate, create, research topics they're interested in, study, and do school work,

Technology is also entertainment for our kids. They might be watching "Try Not to Laugh" videos, make-up or DIY tutorials, or "famous" gamers. They may also be watching educational videos about things we never had access to as kids.

This is our kids' world today. These are not bad things. What they need is our understanding and support to help them to balance, manage, and handle technology responsibly.

Understand That Was Then, This Is Now

We moan and complain a lot about our kids' technology. However, I want to challenge us to look at it from our kids' perspective and help us normalize it a little bit.

When I was growing up, I would stretch the telephone cord down the hallway and into my bedroom behind closed doors. I would talk for hours, and my mom would bang on the door telling me it was time to hang up. I'd yell back, "Give me five more minutes!" only to have her come back twenty minutes later to bang on the door again.

When we were kids, depending on your age, we watched Happy Days, Full House, or Family Matters.

YouTube has replaced those after school sitcoms that we watched as kids.

Gaming is the new Dungeon and Dragons or Kick the Can.

Just like we talked about our favorite TV shows with our friends, our kids watch YouTube videos, or follow Instagrams and Tik-Toks, and talk about them at school. They feel the need to catch up, and watch the same ones so they can be a part of the conversation with their friends.

Gaming is the latest sport - and our gaming kids are competitive. They want to be the best (or at least not be the first one to die) when they are playing against their friends. It's actually on ESPN now!

And remember when we used to pass notes in class? They text or DM (direct message). Did we want our parents reading our private notes? No. They were private and between our friends. It's the same with our kids' texts.

CHAPTER 3

How to Minimize The Challenges (And Arguments) When Setting Limits

"As parents, one of the most important things we can do is regularly evaluate our family priorities to determine whether we are truly living life in accordance with what we say and believe to be important." Amy Carney

Identify Your Goals And Values

It's important to understand what the goal is when it comes to our tweens' and teens' technology.

We want to instill healthy values and give them the tools they need to increase self-awareness. If they have these valuable skills in place, and understand why limits are so important, it will teach them to make wise decisions as they move towards adulthood.

Clarify Your Beliefs

We can feel so reactive around our kids' technology that we don't pause long enough and take the time to get clear about the *what and why* when it comes to navigating our tweens' and teens' technology.

Here are a few questions for reflection. I encourage you to get out a piece of paper and jot down your answers.

What's your biggest area of concern/angst?

What values do you want to cultivate and uphold in your family?

What are the main reasons (your why) behind the limits and ground rules you want to set?

What answers do you need to move forward and be proactive?

Your answers to these questions will help you define your values, set technology ground rules, and understand the positive outcomes you want.

Consider Their Maturity Level

Screen Time Is More than Just Setting Limits

One of the most common questions that I'm asked is *"At what age do I allow my kid(s) to get a smartphone or tablet?"*

Rather than focusing on age, ask yourself real questions concerning the emotional maturity and well-being of your child, separate from their media use.

Questions to ask:

Is my child generally happy?

Is my child physically healthy and sleeping enough?

Is my child socially engaged with family and friends (in any form)?

Is my child putting forth effort and doing well in school?

Is my child pursuing interests and hobbies (in any form)?

Is my child having fun and learning in their use of digital media?

Is their behavior positive during and after watching TV, playing video games, or hanging out online?

Can they keep track of their belongings, or are they regularly losing things?

Do they follow your rules and directions?

Do they exhibit self-control?

Do they spend time with friends and have activities they participate in?

Do they have the maturity to know that not everything they see online is a realistic picture of people, relationships and life?

Are you ready to invest the energy in having these important ongoing conversations, ready to set limits to keep your kids safe?

Define Your Values With The End Goal In Mind

Take An Eagle's Eye View

When we focus on setting limits, it's helpful to take an eagle's eye view. What I mean by an eagle's eye view is stepping back, reflecting on the bigger picture and asking yourself some vital questions.

I want you to imagine for a moment when your teenager leaves your home, what kind of a relationship would you like to have?

What values would you like to have instilled in them?

What memories would you like them to have?

How would you like to have prepared them as they go into the big, wide world?

What character traits do you want to have modeled and cultivated?

Focus on a Few Goals

I encourage you to identify what matters the most to you when it comes to your kids and your family. Write down your goals and keep them nearby.

When it comes to deciding what your expectations, limits and rules will be, you can use this as a guide to help you align with what you want for your kids and your family.

CHAPTER 4

Communication is KEY

Start By Listening

"There is a reason we were created with one mouth and two ears."

Communication is the key to having a great relationship with our kids and provides a strong foundation for them to grow and become responsible, well-adjusted adults.

Communication starts with listening and being open to hearing what the other person has to say. I'm confident that we've all experienced someone in our lives demanding we do something, with no apparent regard for how we're feeling or what we want. If you're like me, these aren't the kinds of people that I want to listen to, nor do I want to comply with their requests. It's the same with our kids.

When it comes to setting limits with your kids around their technology, start by creating an open dialogue. Be a parent whom your tween or teen feels like they can talk to without fear of judgment.

How do you do this?

You get your kids' input when it comes to setting limits versus laying down the law.
You ask good questions and allow them to share their thoughts, opinions, and feelings when it comes to setting limits.
You are accepting and non-judgmental when they share their answers. Avoid criticism.

When you get your kids involved you are showing them that you care what they have to say; their thoughts and viewpoints matter to you. As a result, you will increase the likelihood that they will comply with the limits. Complete parent-driven control, on the other hand, tends to backfire and cause rebellion, lying, and sneaking.

Sample questions that invite parent-teen dialogue:

How do you think screen time should fit into our lives and your life?
What do you think are positive ways to spend time online and

why? Ask them about apps, videos, or websites they enjoy.

Why might it be important to find balance and have limits?

What do you think are some of the negative effects of technology?

How much time do you think is appropriate when it comes to homework and balancing activities?

Do you think social media is getting in the way of doing other things like - spending time with friends, exploring other interests, being physically active, schoolwork, or participating in activities?

What are some of your favorite things to do with your friends online and face-to-face?

Do you have friends you consider close but you mostly interact with online?

Who would you like to spend more time with in person?

Be Humble

For many of us, if we're honest, our reactivity towards our kids' technology may in fact be an excellent example of "the pot calling the kettle black."

It's easy to focus on the amount of time my teen uses technology, but if I'm honest, I am not much better. I get distracted by work deadlines, blog writing, emails, looking at Facebook, texting, and the list goes on. Rather than being so critical of my kids and the ways they are absorbed with technology, I can own the fact that I am easily distracted by technology as well.

When we embrace being humble, less judgmental, and more willing to admit our struggles with having a healthy balance between online and offline time, our kids will be more receptive to what we have to say when we discuss setting limits around our technology.

Consider Yourself A "Media Mentor" Rather Than An Internet Cop

Help your children see screen time as a tool to connect, create, and learn. This positions you as the good guide who wants your kids to get the most out of screen time instead of presenting yourself as the bad cop who wants to take it all away.

Reflect On The Positive Opportunities Technology Offers

You have heard the old adage, "If you can't beat them, join them."

A new study out of Brigham Young University said that teens who are connected with their parents on social media feel closer to them in real life.

We need to reframe our perspective from *technology is the problem* to *technology can offer us positive opportunities to connect our kids and have fun.*

How do you do this?

You look for creative ways to use social media that benefits your relationship with your kids.

Here are a few ideas to use technology positively as a family:

- ❑ Learn something new together
- ❑ Play a video game together
- ❑ Find an on-line recipe and make a meal together
- ❑ Make Pinterest boards
- ❑ Make a music video
- ❑ Use funny face apps to snap pictures or trade faces
- ❑ Look up a tutorial to learn how to do something new
- ❑ Look up funny apps and take turns sharing your creative finds
- ❑ Start a TikTok channel together
- ❑ Find a few YouTubers you can both follow
- ❑ Follow each other on Instagram
- ❑ Facetime a relative faraway
- ❑ Use digital wristbands to encourage everyone to be active
- ❑ Find an app to express creativity with photos, music, coloring, making funny voices, or creating your own movies

Believe In Your Kids' Ability To Make Good Decisions

It's important to reflect on the messages we're sending our kids when it comes to our approach towards them and technology. Are we conveying we don't trust them even when they've proven to be trustworthy?

And if they are breaking the rules, are we curious as to why that might be? Do we get their input and talk about how they can win back trust?

When it comes to your kid's technology, remember to convey the message, *"I believe that you have that wisdom inside of you to make good decisions. I trust you to do that."*

When you believe in your kids' ability to make good decisions, this may be one of the greatest motivations for them to do just that.

Use A Contract

"What we need to do is empower our kids to make good decisions with this new gadget—to help them understand that a cell phone, like all privileges, is a responsibility." Josh Shipp

Whenever your child has the privilege of using a device, it should also come with an accompanying agreement...a contract.

Kids need boundaries and to know what expectations and rules are.

Contracts work best, particularly when your child has a say in the terms of the contract vs. having the rules imposed upon him/her.

At the end of the book, you will find our Moms of Tweens and Teens Cell Phone Contract that you can use as a guide to start the conversation. A cell phone contract helps you be clear about what the guidelines are in order to set limits and keep your child safe.

Whether you have a tween or teen, you can use this Cell Phone contract to encourage a discussion around expectations and limitations on cell phone and social media usage.

Page one is suitable for all ages. For an older child, you may decide to use page 2 as well, which covers sexting and pornography on the web.

As we were told by an officer we interviewed, we should never assume our kids don't know something or that one of their friends won't expose them.

You will find our Cell Phone Contract in the Resources Section.

CHAPTER 5

Decide On Ground Rules

"Kids don't have the big-picture perspective that parents have, so we need to help them cultivate their own sense of self-regulation." Jason Brand, LCSW

There Is No One Size Fits All

In an effort to help families curb kids' technology use, groups such as the American Academy of Pediatrics (AAP) and the World Health Organization (WHO) have released numerical screen limit guidelines, but the reality is that there really is no magic number that's "just right."

Setting screen-time limits - and helping kids moderate their own habits - is all about finding the right balance for your family's needs and lifestyle.

It's important you find what works for you and your family. Even within a family, what works for one kid may not work for another.

Each family dynamic is different. Every family has a different definition of what it means to have "healthy" or positive technology habits. We also must be prepared for rules to change as our kids get older.

Try different things and find what feels right for your family.

Here are some examples of goals you might have for your family around technology:

> I want to use technology to learn and improve our lives.

> I want our family to have balance regarding screen time and other activities (getting outside, being with friends and family, excercise, unplugged downtime, sleep).

> I want my kids to learn to communicate in positive ways online and offline.

> I want face-to-face time with my kids/family - having family night and fun together.

Ask the Important Questions And Get On The Same Page

> *"I'll see your toddler tantrum and raise you a teen*
> *who just had their phone taken away."*

One of the hardest things about parenting tweens and teens and trying to navigate their technology is dealing with the fighting, the push back, and the power struggles. We are trying to be good parents who do what's right, who keep our kids safe, and who enforce limits - all while feeling like we're swimming against the current. It's a continuous, exhausting daily battle that is constantly changing.

Here are some questions to ask yourself and your spouse/partner and discuss with your kids:

Who's going to pay for the cell phone? What are you willing to pay for?

Is it okay for your tween or teen to have the phone in the area where they study?

Will you allow the phone in the bedroom? How about when they're supposed to be sleeping?

Is it ok or not ok for them to use the phone and social media to connect with friends when they first wake up?

Can your tween or teen use social media before they go to bed? When do you expect them to turn it off?

Is it okay to check your child's phone without asking or will you tell them you are going to check it?

Use Your Values To Define Your Ground Rules

I want you to take the values you hold dear and what values you'd like to model, cultivate and uphold in your family and reflect on how these apply when it comes to setting limits, rules and agreements.

Here are a few examples of what this might look like:

Value - Making time for face-to-face connection and downtime

Ground Rule - Phone-free zones

Enforce certain days/times when they must put their phones down for a few hours (which means Mom & Dad too). Movie night, trips to Starbucks, shopping, baking, family dinners and studying can and should be done without a phone in hand. While you may hear some initial complaining, these "phone-breaks" are a great way to show your teens that they can survive without their phone or social media.

Value - Getting Good Sleep

Ground Rule - Phone off at 10

No exceptions. And better yet, no phone before bed.

A major cause of teenage depression is the lack of sleep our teens get. A huge reason for this is smartphones. Not only does the light cause our kids' brains to stay awake, but many studies suggest scrolling social media before bed can increase anxiety and depressive thoughts.

Ensure your teen charges their phone in a room other than their bedroom. In extreme circumstances, shut the home WiFi off at a specific, predetermined time.

◆ ◆ ◆

Value - Safety

Ground Rule - Get the log-in

Many parents often struggle with the moral issue of spying on their kids, which is why I suggest not doing it.

However, possessing the logins is the same as wearing a seat belt in an automobile. Just like the seat belt is a layer of protection from an automobile crash, accessing social media protects tweens and teens online.

Encouraging Cooperation

It's helpful when it comes to encouraging cooperation to include your tween or teen in setting the limits and coming up with consequences. But first, you need to identify the problem and talk about it.

This isn't always easy to know how to do.

Sometimes a great way to do this is to identify a problem - for example - your son is playing Fortnight and when you tell him to get off, he doesn't. You find your frustration rising: you wind up yelling and a full blown argument ensues.

What can you do instead?

I find this to be an effective approach when it comes to setting limits and minimizing conflict while encouraging co-operation.

Note: You want to pick a good time to have this discussion.

You: I'm noticing _____(express the problem) "I'm noticing you're on Fortnight for over 4 hours a day. When I tell you it's time to get off you don't listen and tell me you'll get off in 5 minutes. I wind up yelling and it turns into an argument.

You: Say what you don't want/share feelings. "I don't want to keep nagging and yelling. And it doesn't feel good when I keep reminding you and you're not listening. And I'm imagining it doesn't feel good to you either."

You: Say what you want. "I want us to come up with a strategy or agreement as to how we can handle this so we're not arguing about this constantly. I don't like it and I know you don't either. I have some thoughts and I'd like to hear what you think."

You: Share your thoughts and talk about what you can do to come to an agreement.

If possible, together come up with a consequence if the limit/ agreement isn't followed.

Let your tween or teen know the consequences they can expect and make sure to follow through (more on that in the next chapter).

Check back in after a week to talk about what is working or not working.

Expect That....

"Take Comfort! There is a light at the end of the tunnel!"

When you set limits and/or decide to use parental controls, expect that they won't like it, at least at first.

They will whine, protest, ask why 10-20 times, and be upset when they run out of time.

Remind yourself why you are setting limits:

You are training them in time management, to self-regulate, and to follow through with their responsibilities.

You are supporting them to embrace other activities (such as clubs, exercise, working, spending face-to-face time with their friends, smelling the roses, or cleaning their rooms).

Be encouraged that after a little time, it will be the new normal:

The questions will stop, things will go well, and you will feel as though you can reward them with extra time sometimes.

With parental controls in place, it will start to run itself as if you have no involvement at all.

Have Positive Incentives

Research tells us that our behaviors are more likely to be changed through positive incentives than deterrents. This is especially true for kids.

We can use technology to teach our kids so many important life skills - time management, exercising self-control, strengthening their problem solving skills, and increasing self-awareness.

And when we catch them making good choices we can come up with positive incentives.

For example, if your son sets a timer and gets off his video game without you asking, then he gets a half an hour extra time over the weekend. If your daughter puts her cell phone in your room on the charger without you reminding her, she gets to pick the restaurant you go to on Friday night.

Incentives affirm our kids for the positive choices they're making and motivate them to keep it up.

Have Consequences

Follow-Through Versus Lecture

When you've clearly communicated the limits and boundaries have been broken, you need to hold your tween or teen accountable by following through with the consequence.

It's important that your tween or teen understand the expectations and limits that you set. Include them in the process; allow them to have their say. Be clear what the consequence will be and when they don't adhere to the limit or boundary, follow through.

Here's an example that might help:

Let's say you set a limit for your son that he can play one hour on his video game after homework is done on a school night and after chores are done - only to find out that he hasn't done his chores. A consequence might be that he loses the video game for the rest of the evening or he loses an hour over the weekend.

Understand they will make mistakes and push the boundaries.

Simply put, this is their job - to test the limits at this age. Instead of wasting your energy getting angry, pat yourself on the back for setting limits that they can push up against. This is how they feel safe.

Don't expect them to like having consequences.

Chances are they will whine and complain. Expect it. Do you enjoy having a consequence such as running out of gas when you forget to fill the tank? Same thing. This is how they learn, and it's uncomfortable.

Hold the line

The biggest yellers and complainers are those who have no boundaries. There is no need to yell when you follow through with a consequence. The consequence does the work for you. When you follow through and hold your tween or teen accountable, you will be taken seriously. They will learn that there are consequences for their choices, either positive or negative.

Remind yourself that they had a choice and you're holding them accountable.

Admit when you make mistakes

Our kids are really perceptive at sensing our inconsistencies in our expectations towards them and our behaviors. Of course, age plays a role in our technology use. However, if you tell your tween or teen that you're not going to do something (or you are going to do something), and you don't do what you say, avoid getting defensive when they point it out. Rather than being defensive, admit your mistake and apologize. It's amazing the difference it makes in our kids' willingness to own their mistakes when we can admit our own.

CHAPTER 6

Encourage Positive Online Behavior

How We Engage With Others

On a regular basis, people share with me how they're having a conflict with someone over a text or email that's gotten out of hand. I encourage them to reach out, pick up the phone or have a face-to-face conversation where they can actually hear the tone of voice and the heart of what the other person is saying.

One of the downsides of technology is it can dull our senses to how our words and behaviors impact others.

Our tweens and teens are especially susceptible to not understanding how their words and actions online or through text impacts other people. And all of these exchanges come at a time when their brains are undergoing reconstruction - they lack impulse control and can be quick to respond without thinking.

It's important to encourage and discuss positive online behavior and what's appropriate and what's not.

Here are a few areas to discuss:

Commenting on social media about personal issues is not really appropriate. Discuss the importance of not saying anything that they wouldn't say to someone's face.

When responding back to someone when they're upset, encourage them to pause. When they do respond, recommend they ask themselves if their comment is kind, constructive, and respectful. If they answer "no" to any of these three areas, then they should take a timeout to think through their response.

Talk about the importance of respecting other points of view and beliefs. Talk about treating people online with the same respect you would give them face-to-face.

Discuss the importance of reporting bullying behavior to you directly instead of engaging with it.

Online Reputation

It's important for your tween or teen to understand how mobile technology can affect their future. Share with them that their online reputation is important. Businesses and colleges are spending time searching social media when they are looking at applicants.

Ask them to think about what messages they might be sending and if that is how they really want others to see them.

CHAPTER 7

Keeping Them Safe

T he Cell Phone Contract at the end of this book will assist you in talking through some of these points I'm going to share here. However, I'm going to exchange the risk of being repetitive here for the benefit of being thorough in addressing the issue of keeping your kids safe.

Here are some ideas to keep your kids safe online:

(NOTE: These guidelines will change as they get older)

#1 Do

Keep the computer in a common area of the home.

Restrict incoming communication with the use of software or programs designed to filter out inappropriate content or predators.

Talk regularly and specifically with them about online issues.

Understand that filtering software isn't always perfect. Our kids can be savvy in getting around the filtering programs we use.

Remind them that they can come to you for help if anything is inappropriate, upsetting, or dangerous without fear of punishment.

#2 Don't

Don't threaten and immediately take the phone away.

Don't over-react. If they're afraid of being punished, they will tend to not tell you. What they need is your support and guidance.

The following rules may help:

Ignore communication from people they don't know.

Report cyber-bullying, threats, or other questionable behavior.

Do not pass along pictures or messages that may be hurtful to another child.

Promote "netiquette" - online polite, respectful behavior.

Ask for help from an adult.

#3 Keep Private

They need to know:

Never give out private information if a stranger could obtain that content.

People aren't always who they say they are. Even someone you meet on social media and chat with for months might be lying about their identity.

Don't post your location publicly.

#4 Be Aware of Dangerous Apps

While some apps may seem benign, you would be surprised to find that there are many that are dangerous to our tweens and teens. The technology is moving so fast that it may seem impossible to keep up. This is why it is so important that we keep ourselves educated. We have to remember that there is never any reason our kids need to be in hidden chat rooms or using anonymous texting. We also need to beware of the apps that help our kids hide things. If they have to hide it, you can bet they shouldn't be doing it.

When appropriate, we should make sure our kids have safety settings on their accounts so bad content is blocked.

It is within our right to periodically check to see what apps they have on their phones. We just don't want to get crazy about it.

At the end of the book, you will find our list of Apps of Concern as resources you can use to set limits, block inappropriate content, and keep them safe.

CHAPTER 8

The Negative Impacts of Social Media

C onstant access to digital devices lets kids escape uncomfortable emotions like boredom, loneliness, or sadness by immersing themselves in video games or social media.

We're now seeing the effects of what happens when an entire generation spends their childhood avoiding discomfort.

Electronics are replacing opportunities to develop mental strength and gain the coping skills they need to handle everyday challenges.

Our kids may feel isolated, sad, or lonely and turn to social media to feel better. For other kids, social media may reinforce feelings of sadness, not quite fitting in, or the pressure to look or be a certain way.

Body Shaming and The Obsession To Look Perfect

Body shaming and the obsession to look perfect has become increasingly common among tweens and teens in recent years.

When I was growing up, I saw the popular girl down the hall at school. I envied her hair, her clothes, and how thin and pretty I thought she was. Then, I went home for the day (or weekend) and put her out of my mind.

Now our kids have Instagram. It's hard for them to get away from the staged, filtered ideal pictures which make people look even "better" than they do in real life. It's easy to fall into the comparison and "not enough" trap on a daily basis.

This unrealistic, fictitious perfect image can lead to low self-esteem, depression, eating disorders, discontent, anxiety and even suicidal thoughts.

Our kids need our help sorting through the false messages and beliefs they can internalize from daily exposure to social media.

FOMO (The Fear Of Missing Out)

About half of teenagers use social media everyday. They may check Instagram or Snapchat dozens (or more!) times a day. While this is how many tweens and teens connect with their friends, it can also leave them feeling stressed out, irritable, and exhausted.

This social media-specific anxiety has a name: FOMO, also known as "fear of missing out."

FOMO comes in many forms:

They feel the stress to constantly keep up. If they don't respond right away, they may worry that a friend will be mad at them.

If they're in a text chain and don't answer, they may think they will be excluded from the group or miss out on a conversation.

They see friends post pictures of getting together and wonder why they weren't invited.

There is something constantly happening all the time, and if they're not online too, then they will miss out. They want to belong and fit in at this age, and it's overwhelming for them to try to keep up with it all.

Parents can help. If you see your kids struggling -- maybe they're always stressed out after being on the phone or they're staying up too late texting -- step in.

What you can do:

Don't judge. Listen instead.

While this can drive us crazy and stress us out when we see our kids obsessed with their phones, remember that this is their social life. It's easy to judge and make these forms of connection today "bad." Remember at this age it is so important to them that they feel like they "belong." They want to fit in. So the more you can understand, listen, and empathize, the more they will open up and talk to you when they're feeling stressed out.

Encourage their offline lives.

Encourage them to find activities that build them up and cultivate confidence and a strong sense of who they are and what makes them unique and feel good about themselves. Have them pick one activity each semester - a club, sports, drama or music, a job, volunteering, etc.

Don't be afraid to set limits on the amount of time they spend on their phone.

Ask questions and listen without judgment.

The Comparison Game and Low Self-Esteem

Teens who have created idealized online personas may feel frustrated and depressed by the gap between who they pretend to be online and who they truly are. The compare themselves and the number of likes they receive.

Don't:

Don't underestimate the role social media plays in the lives of teenagers.

Don't dismiss or minimize your tween or teen's experiences. For them, things like the number of likes, negative comments, breakups, or being left out brings up feelings that are very real to them.

Do:

Encourage them to think about social media in a more critical way. Some of the questions below can help you to have these conversations.

Questions to Invite Them Into:

- ❑ *How does social media make you feel?*
- ❑ *What do you like? What don't you like?*
- ❑ *Do you think your friends are really the people they appear to be online?*
- ❑ *How do you want people to perceive you on social media? Why?*
- ❑ *What do you think are some of the downsides of social media?*
- ❑ *What makes a good photo?*
- ❑ *What is it about getting "likes" that feels good?*
- ❑ *How does posting and looking at social media affect your mood?*
- ❑ *What apps do you like best?*
- ❑ *What would happen if you turned off your phone for an hour (or 2) a day? How might you feel?*
- ❑ *What are the pros and cons of using Instagram and other social-networking apps?*
- ❑ *What would happen if you unfollowed or unfriended someone who was making you feel bad on social media?*

CHAPTER 9

The Risks

CyberBullying

The definition of cyberbullying is "the spreading of embarrassing, humiliating, harassing, or damaging communication via the internet or via cell phones by text or picture messages."
The effects of cyberbullying can have devastating consequences.

It can result in a child who faces the struggle of anxiety, emotional pain and trama, low self-esteem, skipping school, damaged friendships, depression, and -in rare cases- suicide.

As parents, we need to be aware that cyberbullying may be happening in our homes without us even knowing it. We must do our best to protect and talk to our kids.

What You Can Do if You Find Out Your Tween or Teen is Being Bullied:

- ❑ Take threats seriously, even if they say "they are joking." Others may not know it's a joke.

- Don't minimize the bullying or tell them to ignore or get over it. The emotional pain of being bullied is very real and can have long-lasting effects.
- Be supportive and understanding.
- Find out how long the bullying has been going on and ensure that you'll work together to find a solution. Let your children know they are not to blame for being bullied.
- Do not retaliate – this only allows the bully to justify his behavior and the victim is seen as contributing to the problem.
- Tell them not to respond to any cyberbullying threats or comments online.
- Don't delete. Instead print out all the messages, take screenshots, online screen names, emails, and any other information available to you. You will need the messages to verify and prove there is cyberbullying.
- Don't threaten to take away their computer or cell phone if they come to you and share a problem. This can lead to them being more secretive.
- Talk to your school's guidance counselors so they can keep an eye out for bullying during the school day.
- Get law enforcement involved if there are threats of physical violence or bullying that continues to escalate.

Sexting

Researchers surveyed 606 teens ages 14-18 and found that approximately 20 percent of the teens said they had sent a sexual image of themselves via cell phone. About twice as many teens admitted to receiving a sext. Of those who reported receiving a sext, well over 25 percent said that they had forwarded it to someone else. So, they're sharing the pics with their friends.

Here's the source https://archive.unews.utah.edu/news_releases/u-study-finds-sending-sexually-explicit-photos-by-cell-phone-more-common-among-teen-than-you-might-think/

Sadly, a third of the teens stated that they didn't think about the legal ramifications or consequences of their actions.

What you can do:

Share real stories in the news to talk about sexting and the consequences.

Discuss peer pressure and normalize the power it can have at this age.

Share with them the consequences -

Legal consequences: In some states, underage sexting can be prosecuted as child pornography. In others, it's treated as a misdemeanor. Either way, it can land your teenager in legal trouble, but many teenagers don't know that. More than 60 percent of students in the Drexel study said they were unaware of the possible legal consequences.

Remind them that once photos are out there you can't get them back.

Go through "what if" scenarios:

- ❑ What if you feel pressured to sext?
- ❑ What if you send a sext and then regret it? Then what happens?
- ❑ What if you break up with your boyfriend/girlfriend—what happens to those pictures?
- ❑ How would you feel if you took a picture and it got passed around?
- ❑ Remind them that once a picture is sent it can never be retrieved.

Talk about pressures to send revealing photos. Let teens know that you understand how they can be pushed or dared into sending something. Tell them that no matter how big the social pressure is, the potential social humiliation can be hundreds of times worse.

Teach your children that if someone sends them a photo, they should delete it immediately. It's better to be part of the solution than the problem.

Emphasize that it is never okay to ask or pressure anyone to sext, nor is it okay to send unsolicited sexts.

Discuss peer pressure and provide strategies for how to say no. Ask them what they might say if someone pressured them and asked them to send a sext.

Make sure they understand that they can come to you with questions or problems NO MATTER WHAT. No matter how inappropriate the content or how embarrassed they feel, they can come to you with no judgement.

What to do if you find sexting photos on your kid's phone:

Be sensitive. As hard as it may be, stay calm and don't react in anger. This can cause them to shut down and not talk to you. Find ways to move beyond the anger before you talk to them.

Stay calm and stay away from catastrophizing.

Tell them what you found and shut up and listen. Let them talk.

Avoid shaming and don't threaten right then and there to take away their phone.

Seek to understand what motivated them to send the sext. Remember the part in this book where I talked about them wanting to fit in and their desire for attention. Oftentimes they are feeling pressured, give in and don't know how to say no. They want attention and to feel special. The desire to be liked can be so strong at this age.

Pornography

"Kids are curious about sex. Spoiler alert: this is normal and healthy. This natural curiosity can, unfortunately, be hijacked by easy-access pornography, which provides highly unrealistic and unhealthy depictions of "sex," and is a low-quality substitute for teaching what real relationships and real intimacy look like."

When it comes to pornography, we can't be naive and think our kids will never see it. If they don't see it on their own device, there is a very good chance they will see it on one of their friends.

So let's operate under the assumption that your kids will come across pornography, whether on purpose or by accident (it's not that hard to mistype into a search engine these days).

Then we need to talk to them about it sooner rather than later.

This is why it is so important to have that open dialogue. Your kids need to know you are a safe place when they see something they are concerned about.

Don't freak out!

We want them to know they won't get into trouble because they saw it, and they won't be shamed or told they are bad or wrong.

If we don't communicate about it or we make our kids afraid of it, our children will be more likely to search it out.

If you haven't, you need to start talking to your kids about sex (see the resources section for some helpful resources).

Your first conversation will set the tone for future conversations, so it's helpful to have a game plan for starting the conversation about pornography.

How to talk to your kids about pornography:

Expect it will be awkward. This is totally normal!

Give them a fair warning — something like,

"We need to talk about Internet pornography; there are a few things I want to be sure you know."

A good way to start to break the ice is, "This is uncomfortable for me to talk about but it's important."

Share what's true - "I know that a lot of kids are looking at porn online, but I'm hoping you won't. Sex can be mutual, loving and fulfilling and it can be dark and destructive. What you see in pornography is almost always the wrong kind of sex, and I don't want you to assume that pornography is what sex is all about."

You might say: "There's another reason I don't want you looking at pornography. People often find that they get turned on by stuff and at the same time they feel bad watching it. I wouldn't want you to experience guilt and shame when something might feel good but in your heart you know it's wrong.

Give them the facts:

Talk about the difference between porn and healthy sex.

What if your teen seems unconcerned about the danger of porn? Many young people are under the misconception that porn is harmless.

Porn is all about taking and abusing, manipulating, and exploiting others.

It sabotages the ability to enjoy normal sex and can lead to keeping secrets, shame, addiction, and serious relationship and marital issues.

Sex in the context of a relationship of intimacy is about giving, serving, loving and sacrificing.

We were designed for intimacy and connection. We were made to love and be loved, to know and be known.

Porn can leave you feeling very lonely, whereas being known and truly loved, respected and valued by another person is so fulfilling.

CHAPTER 10

*How Do You Know If You
Should Be Concerned?*

I f you see any cause for concern, including mood swings that seem to result from social media, a lack of pleasure in activities he or she used to enjoy, and having accompanying symptoms such as headaches and stomachaches, visit your kid's pediatrician for a professional opinion.

Here are the most common symptoms of social media anxiety disorder (http://etec.ctlt.ubc.ca/510wiki/Social_Media_Anxiety_Disorder):

- Interrupting conversations to check your social media accounts
- Lying to others about how much time you spend on social media, gaming and Youtube
- Withdrawal from friends and family
- Trying to stop or reduce your use of media more than once before without being successful

- Loss of interest in other activities
- Neglecting work or school to comment on social media or watch a YouTube video.
- Experiencing withdrawal symptoms when you are not able to access social media or video games
- Spending over six hours per day on social networking sites like Facebook, Twitter, Instagram or YouTube and video games
- Overwhelming need to share things with others on social media sites
- Having your phone with you 24 hours a day to check your social media sites or watch YouTube
- Using social media more often than you planned
- Severe nervousness or anxiety when you are not able to check your notifications
- Negative impacts in your personal or professional life due to social media usage

CHAPTER 11

Gaming

O nline gaming has become one of the most popular ways for kids to play, but it can also be a concern for parents or a source of tension within families. The following guide can help you and your kids agree on positive ways to game.

Explore the Good Parts of Gaming

Have your kids talk about the healthy aspects about the games they play. As a prompt, ask about specific elements often found in gaming, such as learning new information, teamwork, and strategy. If you're game savvy yourself, it might also be helpful to talk about specific aspects of games that you think are positive.

The Not So Good Parts Of Gaming

Now ask them if there are ever times where gaming makes them feel bad or causes conflict with family or friends.

Have they ever encountered bullying or threatening language while playing a game?

This is also a good time to talk about feeling "left out" if they don't play a certain game or if they have to log off before finishing a level.

Brainstorm Positive Ways To Game

Talk about ways gaming can benefit your kids when done in a balanced way. Maybe gaming can help them improve at a sport because they better understand the strategies. Maybe it can help with hand-eye coordination or reflexes. Or maybe it can inspire an offline activity with their friends.

Play Games Together

Gaming comes in many different forms — some may be more positive than others. To better understand the nuances of your kid's games, try playing as a family.

Understand Online Gaming

Many games can now be played against other people (including strangers). Consider this in relation to your kid's level of maturity and ability to judge who they should be engaging with.

CHAPTER 12

Being Intentional - Face-Time Versus Screen Time

"Miss your teens? Turn off the wifi and they will come pouring out of their rooms faster than you can say, "I don't know what happened."

Provide Family Fun Alternatives

Helping your child manage their mobile technology use is much easier when your child has alternatives. Sometimes the best ways to provide alternatives is to have family activities that are fun and entertaining for the whole family.

Think outside of the box. What are some activities that are fun and different that we can do with our kids? I have a friend who recently took her girls on the el-train to a museum in downtown Chicago — just for the pure adventure of it.

Get your kids to come up with a list of fun activities they'd like to try or do and stick it on the refrigerator and check it off.

Get everybody on board by allowing your kids a turn to suggest the next activity.

I have learned to be persistent. Often my kids will initially balk at my ideas yet change their tone after the fact. Recently I went on an adventure with my daughters who fought me tooth and nail, only to have them thank me later for the fun day.

Take Ten

Taking time to connect with your teen doesn't have to be stressful or a big deal. I know my kids feel uncomfortable when I come at them with this type of energy. I find ten minutes a day is a good touch point to start with. We can ask our kids to put away their cell phones during the ride to school or practice. When our kids are adolescents, think quality, not quantity.

Seize The Moment When An Opportunity Presents Itself

When seemingly out of the blue, one of my kids starts to talk to me, I have to remind myself to stop, look and listen. I literally say to myself, "Quit washing dishes, put the phone down, and turn away from your laptop. Stop!" It's not easy for me to transition when I am "in the zone." It takes a conscious reminder that this is a precious moment and I need to seize the opportunity.

Be Present And Enjoy Your Kids

I strive to be someone my kids want to talk to and be with. Yes, It's true, I am not their first choice. And I also have to be curious about why they might not want to talk to me. When I stop to think about it, I don't know if I would like to talk to me when I am with my kids. I try to slip in a teaching moment or start lecturing. I have found when I can lighten up and enjoy myself, they want to talk to me.

Provide Downtime

Kids need to have unstructured time, and technology adds an additional layer to our kids not getting downtime to just *be*.

These days, kids don't have the opportunity to be bored, relax and just play.

While developing interests, talents and hobbies are a good thing and play an important role in kids' lives, many kids today are overscheduled with organized teams and clubs.

Make sure you give your kids unstructured time to be alone, even if they complain about being bored. They need the space to watch the clouds go by, to be present with themselves, and learn how to be comfortable in their own skin.

DISCUSSION QUESTIONS FOR YOU AND YOUR TWEEN OR TEEN

T hese discussion questions are intended to build a stronger relationship with your kids. They will know that you care and want to hear their thoughts, feelings, and what they have to say.

You are laying a foundation to increase the likelihood that they will feel safe to come and talk to you if they are having an issue or are exposed to inappropriate content.

These questions will also help your tween or teen to become more self-aware and strengthen their self-monitoring skills.

When you have these discussions, it's important to withhold judgement and remember the bigger vision of creating a strong relationship for years to come.

Questions to help you get clear first:

- What's your biggest areas of concern/angst?
- What values do you want to cultivate and uphold in your family?
- What are the main reasons (your why) behind the limits and ground rules you want to set?
- Where might you need to educate yourself?
- What answers do you need to move forward and be proactive?
- Why do you care how much time your kids spend on their screens?

Other questions to consider:

- Who's going to pay for the cell phone? What are you willing to pay for?

- Is it okay for your tween or teen to have the phone in the area where they study?

- Will you allow the phone in the bedroom? If so, all the time? How about when they're supposed to be sleeping?

- Are devices allowed at the table? Breakfast? Dinner?

- Is there a time when screens should be put away?

- What time will screens/phones be turned off? Where will the phone or tablets sleep for the night?

- Is it ok or not ok for them to use the phone and social media to connect with friends when they first wake up?

- Can your tween or teen use social media before they go to bed? When do you expect them to turn it off?

- Is it ok to check your child's phone without asking or should you tell them you are going to check it?

When and how will we use devices?

Tweens and teens who are included in the decision making process are more likely to comply with the limits. This doesn't mean you have to make your limits solely based on their input. The goal here to to let them know what they think matters to you.

- *Where should devices go at night and when you're not using them?*

- *Where should you go and not go online?*

- *What can you do to stay safe and private online?*

- *What consequences should there be if you break our online safety rules? What should you do if you see something online that upsets you?*

How should social media fit into our daily lives?
How does it impact us?

- *What are our family values? Values as individuals?*
- *How do you think screen time should fit into our lives - your life and as a family?*
- *How much time do you think is appropriate when it comes to homework and balancing activities?*

- *Do you think social media is getting in the way of doing other things - spending time with friends, exploring other interests, being physically active, school work, or participating in activities?*

How might social media contribute to how we feel?

- *How does social media make you feel?*
- *What do you like? What don't you like?*
- *What do you like about Instagram or your video game?*
- *How do you feel when you're looking at other people's Instagram feeds?*
- *How do you feel when you're gaming or done gaming?*

How might social media affect us and others being present?

- *Do you remember a time when you distracted and you missed something because you were on your phone?*
- *Have you experienced others (friends or family) not being fully present with you? How did that feel?*
- *Have you missed something significant because you were distracted by technology. How did you feel afterwards?*

As a Family: What times and places do we agree it's important to be focused and present with one another?

When is it important that you/we be focused? During homework? When we're together as a family? During chores? At dinner?

What changes do we need to make that would create more balance in our family and as individuals?

Is there a time in the day when we'd like to unplug and be together?

Getting to Know What They Like/Creating Connection:

- *What apps do you like best?*
- *What's your favorite YouTube channel?*
- *What's your favorite video game?*
- *Can you show me? Tell me more about what you like about it.*

Discussing the dangers with them:

- People aren't always who they say they are. Even someone you meet on social media and chat with for months might be lying about their identity. Don't post your location publicly.

- If someone, even a friend, makes you feel uncomfortable, tell me about it. We'll discuss what we need to do about it, and I won't make any decisions about it without your input.

- Don't share any nude or suggestive photos with anyone, even if you know and trust the person. Sometimes these photos get stolen or intentionally shared or posted publicly.

Get their thoughts on the matter:

- ❑ Does technology ever prevent you from being present?
- ❑ Tell me about that app.
- ❑ Here's A List Of Dangerous Apps...What Do You Think? Do You Recognize Any On The List?
- ❑ Here's A Cell Phone Contract - What don't you like? What do you think is fair/unfair?

Talk about the challenges:

- ❑ Talk about how devices can sometimes cause people to miss out on things that matter to them. Touch on the times when you weren't fully "there" because you were on your phone.
- ❑ Talk about what your own goals are regarding social media and if they think they could benefit from setting a goal for themselves.

Talk about how they think social media impacts their friendships:

- ❑ Do you think social media has made our society more social or less social?
- ❑ What are some of your favorite things to do with friends online? Face-to-Face?
- ❑ Do you have friends you consider close but you mostly interact with online?
- ❑ Who would you like to spend more time with in person?

Special Article From Our Moms of Tweens and Teens Blog

"Should I Read My Kid's Texts?"

This week I sat down to research and compile a list of the best apps for protecting our kids on their cell phones, when I came upon an article entitled, "5 Best Apps for Spying on Your Teen."

This title didn't sit well with me.

Now, who of us hasn't read our kid's texts? I know I have and I've found out a lot of valuable information that I wouldn't have discovered if I hadn't.

Reading my kid's texts has left me feeling proud, horrified, validated and more anxious than before I started.

I've felt proud when they've shown such maturity and wisdom in their responses when their friends have texted them with their problems.

I've been surprised and laughed out loud at their wit and humor.

I've had the wool yanked from my eyes and seen through my rose-colored glasses to what was really going on.

My gut instincts have been validated.

"Yep, that kid's trouble."

"Yep, they weren't telling the truth."

"Yep, I need to say no to that sleepover."

"Yep, there's drinking going on."

We have a laundry list of valid reasons for reading our kid's texts...

"It's my right as the parent; I'm paying for the darn thing."

"There's cyber-bullying and it's a scary world out there, it's my job to protect my child and to keep them safe."

"If they're drinking, doing drugs or looking at pornography I need to know about it."

"At the very least I want to know if they've arrived safely at their destination."

"God forbid how guilty I'd feel if I didn't know they were being cyber-bullied, sexting, doing drugs, or a creepy person was talking to them!"

Monitoring our kids cell phones is just part of being a good parent, in a digital age right?

Not so fast.

I'm here to challenge us to not answer yes so quickly.

Now, lest you start pointing your finger at me lecturing me about all the dangers, let me just say, I'm fully aware the struggle is real!

While I'm an advocate in being proactive to protect our kids, I want us to examine our reasons a little further before we download our monitoring apps and read our kid's texts.

Every time I hear about a mom that is reading her kids texts nightly I have a strong reaction.

I've been that mom and I regret it.

Yes, you're hearing me right – if you're reading their texts every night, I'm challenging you to stop it.

With my oldest, texting hadn't been invented. MySpace was the thing at the time.

I was scared (freaking out better describes it). My teen was hanging with the "wrong" crowd and I didn't know what to do.

I wanted to know what was going on so I could protect my kid from bad things happening.

So, I downloaded an app (it was called a *program* at the time with a DVD to download) and I was sent daily emails that shared every comment and conversation.

My choice to download that program was not a good thing. In fact, it caused greater distress and problems.

One of the reasons I'm so passionate about this topic is that I've experienced the damage it does to our relationships when we parent from a place of **fear and anxiety**.

When fear is in the driver's seat, ultimately it's not going to steer you in the right direction.

Reading my daughter's texts didn't protect her, or keep bad things from happening. In fact, it hurt my relationship with my daughter.

The more I read my daughter's conversations the more my over-the-top my reactions became, the more over-the-top my reactions became, the less my teen wanted to talk to me and the more suspicious I became.

My fear got worse and the distance between us became greater.

Here are 5 questions to ask yourself as you wonder if you should read your tween or teen's texts.

Are you putting your relationship first?

I never thought about this back in my teen's MySpace day.

When an adolescent gets the message that you're infringing on their privacy and overly involved in their life, it will cause a rift in your relationship.

One of the most important things we can ask ourselves as parents is what I'm doing conducive to creating a closer relationship.

I'm not saying we are to be our kids' friends....what I'm challenging us to think about is this: what are the consequences of potentially damaging the trust in your relationship?

More than anything else, parenting is about *relationship*. After coaching moms for over a decade, I've learned that many of the parenting issues we struggle with stems from a disconnect in the relationship. When we focus on our relationship first, we increase the chances that our kids will listen to what we have to say.

Are you checking your kid's texts because you're driven by fear, or do you have valid reasons?

I remember as a teen stretching the hallway phone cord as far as I could to get the phone into my room and shutting the door. If my mom would have listened in to my conversations as a teen I'm sure she would have probably gone nuts and not let me go out of the house.

There's just some stuff that is better for us to not know about.

Much of our teens' conversations are innocent talk fueled by the fact that they're trying to figure out who they are.

Our teens need space.

We're a generation of parents who are way too overly involved and into our kids business because *we are parenting by fear*.

I can understand checking texts more often when we're concerned about our kids doing drugs, or something being amiss and they're not talking, or heeding the signs that they're in potential danger.

We need to know the difference between parenting by fear and being a responsible parent.

What does it mean to be a responsible parent when it comes to our kids' cell phones?

How much monitoring is too much? Where do we draw the line?

We need to be aware of *when we're reacting rather than being proactive.* We need to talk about the tough topics and our expectations and rules surrounding their smartphones.

What We Need To Do To Be Responsible Parents

I like what Josh Shipp says, "*What we need to do is empower our kids to make good decisions with this new gadget—to help them understand that a cell phone, like all privileges, is a responsibility.*"

We should stay informed about the apps that we don't want on our kid's phones.

We should make sure our kids have safety settings on their accounts so bad content is blocked.

And it is within our right to periodically check to see what apps they have on their phones, we just don't want to get crazy about it.

Discuss the dangers, cyberbullying, sexting and the misuse of texting and internet access.

A **cell phone contract** can be a great tool to be intentional to discuss our rules and talk about being responsible.

What's the message we're sending our kids when we read their texts?

The most damaging message I was sending my teen was, *"I don't trust you,"* and *"You're bad,"* when I was constantly reacting out of my fear.

I can't stress enough the power we have in our kids' lives over who they grow up to believe they are.

When we believe in our kids' ability to make good decisions, chances are they will.

I still catch myself when I'm saying something that is not sending my youngest, also a teen, the message that I believe in her and trust her to make good decisions.

> *I tell her often, "I believe that you have that wisdom inside of you to make good decisions. I trust you to do that."*

Try it. There is a change in their whole demeanor. *You can see them taking it in and standing a little taller.*

Are we looking for information because our kid isn't

communicative?

Being less communicative is part of being a teen. As moms, this is unsettling.

I've found myself peeking at texts not out of a place of concern; rather I want to know what's going on because they tell me so little.

I've had moms share how they read their teens' texts because they're concerned about their social lives and if they have any friends - which only leads them to ask their teens unhelpful questions. They've decided to stop it and so have I.

It's difficult but we need to resist doing this.

CONCLUSION

I implore you to not go right to reading their texts because we're parenting out of fear and bypassing the most important things. Let's not allow fear to get in the way of building stronger relationships with our teens.

Let's instead be proactive to stay informed, set up house rules and be discerning on what it means to keep them safe in our digital world.

More importantly, let's talk to our kids and build stronger relationships with them first. Let's have the important discussions and find opportunities to connect so we know how they're doing.

Let's take them out to lunch and carve out intentional time.

RESOURCES TO PROTECT YOUR KIDS

I don't believe in spying or sneaking your child's phone out of their bedroom either—but I also don't think handing over what's basically a *super-charged portal to the Internet* is smart either. Coupling this with my lack of tech savvy, I've struggled with giving sound product recommendations to my clients.

Sanity isn't about "watching" what they are doing on their phones, instead it's about safety and managing how they use them.

PROGRAMS TO SET LIMITS, MANAGE AND PROTECT YOUR KIDS

Parental Controls That We Recommend:

Different tech solutions and programs are appropriate for different situations.

Don't be afraid to dig in. All of these programs that we recommend have very robust customer service (that's a huge reason why we choose them!). Their goal is to make sure that you succeed.

Also, don't be afraid to mix and match solutions. Not every solution will be the perfect fit. Sometimes you need a combination, e.g. you can use Screentime and Disney Circle and Xbox built-in controls.

Using a monitoring service is helpful to setting limits and protecting your kids but there is one thing that is more effective than any program you will have and it's free.

It's you.

Digital tools and settings can help you stay on top of your kid's online life, but they can't replace staying involved, having conversations, and helping them make responsible choices.

iPhone or iPad

Screentime, the newest setting by Apple, is by far the most effective way to control your child's usage of their iPhone or iPad (this is not an app).

You can:

Create Downtime - You can have multiple downtimes, for homework or bedtimes, etc. You can even have different downtimes on different days.

App Limits - these are time limits and downtimes for specific apps.

Always Allowed - Say you want your child to have no access to any apps on their phone when they go to bed, but you do want them to have access to the Calm app because it helps them sleep. This app would go into the "Always Allowed" category.

Content & Privacy restrictions - This is just what you think it is with very robust choices to filter content and create rules about how they can use their phone.

Find out more about these settings

Specific   Instructions: https://support.apple.com/en-us/HT201304

Android

We have found the two most effective ways to control and monitor your child's screen time and to keep them safe are these two programs, neither are actual apps, so they cannot be deleted. All of these controls can be done remotely, you do not need access to your child's device beyond initial setup.

Circle Go

Works for Android and Apple (this requires the purchase of the Circle device, but we will explain why you want that in the next section). Circle gives you a bird's-eye view of all things internet. Review your family's online time, site visits, app usage, even the current location of your kids.

Time Limits: Time limits for specific apps and categories.

OffTime - You can have multiple offtimes, for homework, car rides, etc. You can even have different offtimes on different days.

Bedtime: this is specific bedtime limits you can different bedtimes on different days.

Filter: This filters out content based on what level you want your child to see. This is a great place to put content restrictions on YouTube, it will also filter out any pornography, suicide related content etc. It is very robust. You can also block specific apps here.

Pause: If at any time you decide your child needs a break, whether it's behavior or a specific event you haven't set up a downtime for, you just hit the pause button and it goes off.

Rewards: If your child deserves some extra time, for any reason, you can add time here.

Usage: You can see where your child's time is spent and how much.

History: You can see the actual web addresses of any site the child has visited.

Netsanity (works for android and apple, but since Screentime is free on apple we are no longer recommending it for apple devices)
App Blocker: Block specific apps.
Time Blocker: You can have multiple offtimes, for homework, car rides and bedtimes all in one place. You can even have different offtimes on different days.
Game Blocker: Block specific games.
Cat Blocker: This blocks specific categories of websites, pornography, online betting, suicide, etc.
Site Blocker: Here you can actually block specific websites based on URL.
YouTube Filtering: Here you can drill down and filter YouTube in very specific ways.
Safe Search: This immediately filters out dangerous content from both Google and Bing.
Time Out: Instantly turns off everything
Disable Texting: *Android only.*
Disable Calls to and from contact list: *Android only.*
Disable All Apps and Games: *Android only.*
See wifi and data usage: *Android only.*
https://netsanity.net/features/

You can find a comparison chart of all three monitoring programs here: https://momsoftweensandteens.com/cell-phone-monitoring-comparison-chart/

Bark

How It Works:

Bark's watchdog engine uses advanced algorithms to look for a variety of potential issues, such as cyberbullying, sexting, drug-related content, and signs of depression.

If a potential issue is detected, a text/email alert is sent to you to review the issue, along with recommended actions on how to handle the situation.

Find out more about Bark here: use this link to receive 2 weeks free. Or go to this URL https://www.bark.us/?ref=TWEENSANDTEENS or use the code TWEENSANDTEENS at checkout.

Direct Control of Programs and Gaming Consoles

Amazon: https://www.amazon.com/gp/help/customer/display.html?nodeId=201423060

Google Play: https://support.google.com/googleplay/answer/1075738?hl=en

HBO Go: https://help.hbogo.com/hc/en-us/articles/204178528-How-to-use-parental-controls-with-HBO-GO

Hulu: https://www.cordcutters.com/how-use-parental-controls-hulu

Netflix: https://help.netflix.com/en/node/264

YouTube Kids: https://support.google.com/youtubekids/answer/6172308?hl=en

For regular YouTube, I have my child use my own account so that I can view history and turn on safe search restrictions.

Controlling WiFi

Disney Circle - Features are the same as the mobile version, but filter the wifi signal.

You purchase the device and there is no monthly fee for wifi control.

https://meetcircle.com/

You can use this in conjunction with Circle Go very seamlessly.

Easily identify which devices are accessing the wifi and attach them to each specific person in your household. Then you can create specific limits for each device. This includes game consoles, Roku's, iPhones, Android, whatever device is accessing your WiFi. Even when your child has friend's over!

Time Limits: Time limits for specific apps and categories.

OffTime: You can have multiple offtimes, for homework, car rides, etc. You can even have different offtimes on different days.

Bedtime: This is specific bedtime limits you can *different bedtimes on different days.*

Filter: This filters out content based on what level you want your child to see. This is a great place to put content restrictions on YouTube, it will also filter out any pornography, suicide related content etc. It is very robust. You can also block specific apps here.

Pause: If at anytime you decide your child needs a break, whether it's behavior or a specific event you haven't set up a downtime for, you just hit the pause button and it goes off.

Rewards: If your child deserves some extra time, for any reason, you can add time here.

Usage: You can see where your child's time is spent and how much.

History: You can see the actual web addresses of any site the child has visited.

Xfinity has built in parental controls.

https://www.xfinity.com/support/articles/set-up-parental-controls-with-comcast-networking

Identify which devices are using your WiFi

Create Bedtime - You can create bedtimes off of specific devices

Pause - You can pause all wifi or specific devices

Block Specific Sites

Block Keywords

Create trusted computers that bypass parental settings.

All other Wifi

This requires a little tech savvy, but through almost all routers you can create a level of security. With most restriction abilities being the same as Xfinity.

https://www.cnet.com/how-to/how-to-use-your-routers-parental-controls/

Gaming Consoles

XBox

These links will allow you to set up time limits, restrict access to adult content, ability to get on the internet, restrict purchases and more.

https://support.microsoft.com/en-us/help/4028244/microsoft-account-set-up-screen-time-limits-for-your-child

https://www.xbox.com/en-US/xbox-one-s/family-

entertainment
https://support.xbox.com/en-US/browse/xbox-one/security
https://support.xbox.com/en-US/xbox-one/security/core-family-safety-features

Playstation

Some of playstation's features are not free.

These links will allow you to restrict access to adult content, ability to get on the internet, restrict purchases, restrict the ability to use it as a blu-ray player and more.

Also create time limits and time restrictions.

https://www.playstation.com/en-gb/get-help/help-library/my-account/parental-controls/play-time-settings/

https://support.playstation.com/s/article/PS4-Parental-Controls?language=en_US

Windows 10

You can control access time on your child's computer using Windows 10 parental controls.

https://kidlogger.net/blog/parental-control-in-windows-10.html

FAMILY CELL PHONE CONTRACT

You can access printable versions of our Cell Phone Contract Here: https://momsoftweensandteens.com/cellphonecontract/

1. I understand that this phone is owned by my parents. The main reasons I am receiving this phone is to communicate with them, and for personal safety.

2. All of my passwords and usernames for my phone, apps and email will be known by us at all times. And you won't be mad if we check your accounts.

3. Appropriate use times are __am - ___pm on weekdays and __am - __pm weekends. At night my phone will be turned off and charged in an agreed upon place.

4. I will not use the phone during homework or mealtimes, or any other times we agree upon.

5. I will not take videos or pictures of people without their permission. I will not use videos or pictures of people because I think they're funny without permission.

6. I will never be mean or hurtful to someone in a text, post or chat. I understand that once I hit send it is out in the world forever. Anyone can screenshot.

7. I will report bullying immediately.

8. I will never accept a friend request or chat request from someone I don't know in real life. I will never tell anyone where I live or post pictures of identifying places. I understand that someone who seems nice in a chat may not be who they say they are. The Stranger Danger rule applies here too.

10. I understand that I am responsible for losing or damaging my phone.

11. I understand that this contract represents trust between me and my parents, and if I break that trust by violating any of these rules, there will be consequences; including, but not limited to, losing my phone privileges.

The following are for older kids:

12. I will not, under any circumstances, take photos of myself not fully clothed or my private parts, or receive pictures of anyone else's private parts.This is illegal.

I understand that any picture I take or that someone else take of me can be screen shotted and shared with anyone in the world at any time.

13. The internet is full of inappropriate images and videos which can be accessed by mobile phones. If you are curious about these things, or have questions, we are here to answer everything.

Understand that the images you find online do not represent "real life."

What your friends tell you "they know" is nonsense and your phone is not the tool to find out – 99% of the time your friends make stuff up to seem cool.

We understand that it might be embarrassing to ask us. But we promise we will never joke or shy away from your questions, and we will give you the info you want.

APPS OF CONCERN

This list is by no means comprehensive. However we have done our best to compile an accurate list, the apps are changing all the time, so the best thing you can do is research what your child is asking to download, and if they can download on their own, be curious! Google apps you don't recognize!

Social Media Apps:
Snapchat
Shots App - The Comedy App
Kik
Whisper - Share, Express, Meet
Foursquare - Find Places to Eat, Drink, and Visit
Tumblr
Instagram
Facebook
Twitter
Wishbone - Compare Anything
FriendO - The Best Friend Game
Yubo (Formerly Yellow)
Telegram
tbh (to be honest) / Lipsi
Houseparty - Group Video Chat
Reddit: The Official App

YouNow: Live Stream Video Chat

Holla - matches with STRANGERS

Sayat.Me - Asks strangers to rate them

LMK

YOLO

Sarahah

Spotafriend - Teen Meeting App to Make New Friends

MeetMe - Chat and Meet New People

UpLive

Apps Used to Hide Things:

Hide It Pro

Vaulty - Hides photos videos and shows who is trying to access the app

Omegle, ChatHub - completely anonymous messaging very high in sexual content

Calorie Counter – Hide My Text

Hide My Text – Invisible

Secret Hidden Calculator Free

GalleryVault Pro Key

Stashword

Private Photo Vault

Best Secret Folder

Games and Entertainment with Hidden Chat and Accessible Inappropriate Content

Animal Jam

Giphy

TikTok (was Music.ly)

Ask.fm
live.ly
roblox
Flinch

OTHER RESOURCES

Helpful Websites:

Cyberwise

ChildMind

Educate Empower Kids

Protect Young Minds

Culture Reframed– Parents Program

Common Sense Media

Sexting Resources:

Common Sense Education's Sexting Handbook.
This resource gives families the language and support to take texting and cell phone power back into their own **hands. It's** also a great resource for parents who are uncomfortable dealing directly with this issue.

Pornography Resources:

Updating "The Talk" With Your Kids About Porn & What To Be Aware Of

"Let's Talk About Porn," an interactive website that can help you have a conversation about porn with virtually anyone—including your kids.

---

[1] Kowalski, R. M., Giumetti, G. W., Schroeder, A. N., & Lattanner, M. R. (2014). Bullying in the digital age: A critical review and meta-analysis of cyberbullying research among youth. Psychological Bulletin, 140(4), 1073

[2] http://journals.sagepub.com/doi/10.1177/2167702617723376

OF TWEENS & TEENS.COM

Raising adolescents in today's world is hard. That's why Sheryl's mission for Moms of Tweens and Teens, is to provide moms in every city nationwide, with a life-giving community where they can share their hearts, be encouraged, support one another and gain the resources they need to build stronger and healthier relationships with their adolescents and families.

MOTTS mission is to provide moms of adolescents with a resource to inspire growth and a community to foster feelings of comfort, support, and sisterhood. MOTTS is committed to raising up the next generation to become life changers and make the world a better place.

Please visit us at MomsofTweensandTeens.com

Sheryl Gould is a Parenting Expert and author who has been coaching moms for over 15 years. She is the founder and CEO of Moms of Tweens and Teens, a national organization supporting moms to grow in their self-awareness, become more effective parents, and build stronger connections with their adolescents and families.

Sheryl loves supporting moms through her international online community, public speaking, writing, and interactive parenting workshops. Sheryl's mission for Moms of Tweens and Teens is to provide all moms a non-judgmental and compassionate place to share the struggles and triumphs of raising teens and tweens. Sheryl speaks to parents on a wide range of topics related to parenting adolescents helping them to build healthier relationships and empowering their kids to thrive.

 Jen Kehl is the COO of Moms of Tweens and Teens. She is passionate about supporting and connecting with moms in this season of their lives because, she is in that fox hole with them. She has a background in psychology which she forgot to use when she started raising her now teenager. She is also a published author, music blogger, food allergy pro, photographer, controller of chaos, and all around interesting person who refuses to put herself into any one category (because that's boring).

Made in the USA
Columbia, SC
13 March 2021